Tina Charles

31

THE STORY OF THE CONNECTICUT SUN

Brionna Jones

WNBA: A HISTORY OF WOMEN'S HOOPS

THE STORY OF THE

CONNECTICUT SUN

JIM WHITING

Renee Montgomery

CREATIVE EDUCATION / CREATIVE PAPERBACKS

Published by Creative Education and Creative Paperbacks
P.O. Box 227, Mankato, Minnesota 56002
Creative Education and Creative Paperbacks are imprints of
The Creative Company
www.thecreativecompany.us

Design and production by Blue Design (www.bluedes.com)
Art direction by Rita Marshall

Photographs by AP Images (Gerald Herbert, Steve Miller), Getty (Rob Carr,
Tim Clayton/Corbis, Icon Sportswire, MCT, Ethan Miller, Michael Reaves, Jeff
Vinnick)

Library of Congress Cataloging-in-Publication Data
Names: Whiting, Jim, 1943- author.
Title: The story of the Connecticut Sun / by Jim Whiting.
Description: Mankato, Minnesota : Creative Education and Creative
    Paperbacks, [2024] | Series: Creative Sports. WNBA : A History of
    Women's Hoops. | Includes index. | Audience: Ages 8-12 | Audience:
    Grades 4-6 | Summary: "Middle grade basketball fans are introduced to
    the extraordinary history of WNBA's Connecticut Sun with a photo-laden
    narrative of their greatest successes and losses"-- Provided by
    publisher.
Identifiers: LCCN 2022034236 (print) | LCCN 2022034237 (ebook) | ISBN
    9781640267183 (library binding) | ISBN 9781682772744 (paperback) | ISBN
    9781640008694 (pdf)
Subjects: LCSH: Connecticut Sun (Basketball team)--History--Juvenile
    literature.
Classification: LCC GV885.52.C66 W55 2024 (print) | LCC GV885.52.C66
    (ebook) | DDC 796.323/6409746--dc23/eng/20220720
LC record available at https://lccn.loc.gov/2022034236
LC ebook record available at https://lccn.loc.gov/2022034237

Printed in China

Chiney Ogwumike

CONTENTS

LEGENDS OF THE HARDWOOD

Taj McWilliams-Franklin, Shannon Johnson and Katie Douglas

BORN IN THE FLORIDA SUN

T he Connecticut Sun trailed the Charlotte Sting by six points in the first game of the first round of the 2003 Women's National Basketball Association (WNBA) Eastern Conference playoffs. Less than two minutes remained.

"I just told them to hang in there and we'd figure something out at the end," said Sun coach Mike Thibault. They did. Power forward Taj McWilliams-Franklin had a four-point play. It narrowed the margin to 66–64. The Sun tied the score moments later. With less than 10 seconds left, Sun small forward Nykesha Sales blocked a shot. She called timeout. Thibault set up a play for McWilliams-Franklin. She scored on a layup. Sales stole the inbounds pass. The Sun won 68–66!

The Sun hadn't risen yet when the WNBA began play in 1997. The league had eight teams. It added two more in 1998. Two more would join in 1999. One would be in Minnesota. The other would be in Orlando, Florida.

LEGENDS
OF THE HARDWOOD

NYKESHA SALES
FORWARD
HEIGHT: 6-FOOT-0
MIRACLE/SUN SEASONS: 1999–2007

FROM AGONY TO ALL-STAR

Near the end of the 1998–99 college season, UConn star Nykesha Sales ruptured her Achilles tendon. She was one point away from the school's all-time scoring record. UConn played Villanova in the next game. The coaches agreed to let Sales set a new record. Kerry Bascom held the existing record. She approved the plan. Villanova allowed UConn to win the opening tip and pass to Sales. She was standing beneath the basket. She scored. UConn let Villanova score an uncontested layup. The game started 2–2 rather than 0–0. Sales was assigned to Orlando as part of the WNBA expansion draft. She was an eight-time All-Star and is the franchise's all-time leading scorer.

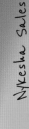

Nykesha Sales

At that time, every WNBA team was affiliated with a National Basketball Association (NBA) team. Orlando's NBA franchise was named Magic. The WNBA team became Miracle.

Expansion teams in pro sports usually lose most of their games in their first season. The Miracle didn't. The American Basketball League (ABL) had begun play in 1996. That was a year before the WNBA. The ABL folded early in 1999. Its best players joined WNBA teams. That provided a solid core of experienced stars for the Miracle. They included Sales, McWilliams-Franklin, and point guard Shannon Johnson.

The Miracle hovered near .500 for most of the season. They fell to 10–16 after a loss to the New York Liberty on August 9. Then they had a five-game winning streak. It boosted them to 15–16. But the Miracle lost to the Detroit Shock in the last game. They finished in a three-way tie for second in the Eastern Conference. Orlando missed the playoffs due to tiebreakers.

The Miracle finished third in the conference in 2000 with a 16–16 record. They earned a spot in the playoffs. Orlando faced the Cleveland Rockers in the first round. The Miracle won the first game of the best-of-three series. Cleveland took the next two.

Orlando began 2001 with a 1–6 mark. They were never in playoff contention and finished 13–19. They started 7–3 in 2002. The 16–16 final mark tied for fourth. Once again, a tiebreaker kept them out of the playoffs.

A major change in league rules was about to take place. It would particularly affect the Miracle.

FROM MIRACLE TO MOHEGAN

WNBA attendance was declining. So were television ratings. The league abandoned the rule that teams had to be affiliated with NBA teams. The Miracle owners decided to sell the team. The Mohegan Tribe in Uncasville, Connecticut, bought it. The tribe owned the Mohegan Sun Casino. The casino included an arena used for concerts, arena football, boxing, wrestling, and other events. The tribe named their new basketball team the Connecticut Sun. They adapted an ancient tribal symbol for the logo.

Other WNBA teams play in major population centers. Uncasville is small, with about 11,000 people. However, it is a short drive from the University of Connecticut (UConn). The school has what many people regard as the best women's college basketball program. Its widespread support helped create a large fan base for the Sun. "We didn't have to explain women's basketball to people," said Sun team official Mitchell Etess. It also helped that two players— Nykesha Sales and center Rebecca Lobo—had played at UConn. They became instant Sun fan favorites.

The team finished in a tie for second in the Eastern Conference in 2003 with an 18–16 mark. It was Mike Thibault's first season as coach. Shooting guard Katie Douglas had been the team's top draft choice in 2001. She provided scoring punch. The Sun faced the Sting in the first round of the playoffs. After the thrilling

Rebecca Lobo

first-game win, Connecticut defeated Charlotte 68–62 in the next game. They won the series. The magic ended in the conference finals. The Shock swept the best-of-three series.

Connecticut finished 18–16 again in 2004. Rookie guard Lindsay Whalen became an instant starter. She averaged nearly five assists a game. The Sun tied for first in the conference with the New York Liberty. They lost the first game of the conference semifinals to the Washington Mystics. The Sun won the next two by double-digit margins. Then they swept the Liberty in the conference finals.

Now they faced the Seattle Storm in the WNBA Finals. The Sun opened up a 16-point second-half lead in Game 1. They held on to win 68–64. The Storm won the next two games to take the title.

The Sun powered to a WNBA-best 26–8 record in 2005. Thibault was named WNBA Coach of the Year. One key was trading for 7-foot-2 center Margo Dydek.

Margo Dydek

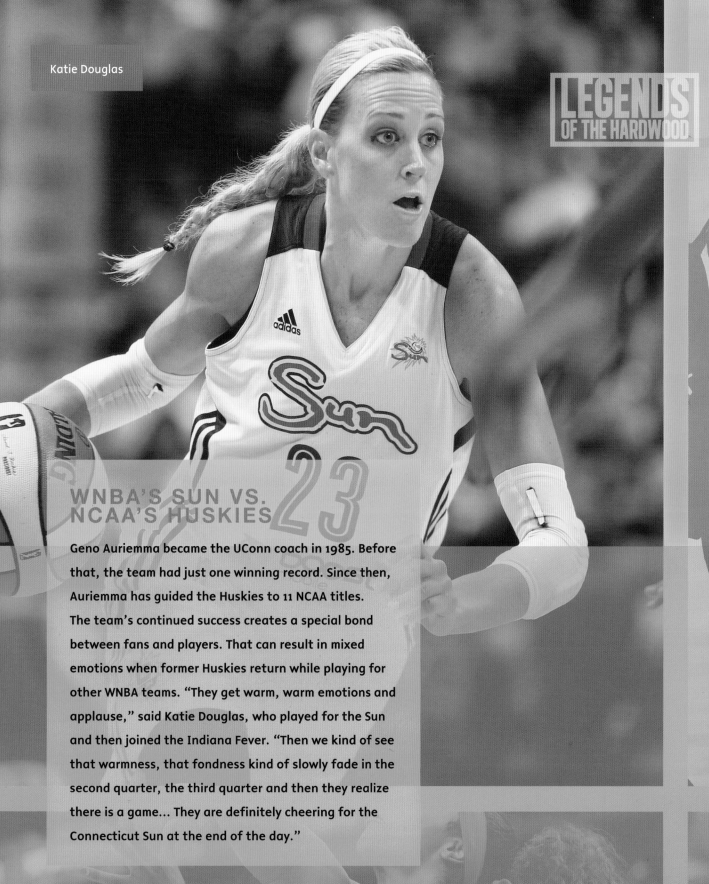

Katie Douglas

WNBA'S SUN VS. NCAA'S HUSKIES

Geno Auriemma became the UConn coach in 1985. Before that, the team had just one winning record. Since then, Auriemma has guided the Huskies to 11 NCAA titles. The team's continued success creates a special bond between fans and players. That can result in mixed emotions when former Huskies return while playing for other WNBA teams. "They get warm, warm emotions and applause," said Katie Douglas, who played for the Sun and then joined the Indiana Fever. "Then we kind of see that warmness, that fondness kind of slowly fade in the second quarter, the third quarter and then they realize there is a game… They are definitely cheering for the Connecticut Sun at the end of the day."

CONNECTICUT SUN

LEGENDS
OF THE HARDWOOD

Asjha Jones

ASJHA JONES
FORWARD
HEIGHT: 6-FOOT-2
SUN SEASONS:
2004–12

FINALLY FINDING HER FOOTING

Asjha Jones began playing basketball at a nearby park when she was just three years old. She reached her adult height when she was 12. She usually played against boys. She towered over most of them in her size-13 shoes. Jones was a McDonald's All-American in high school. She played college basketball at UConn. The Washington Mystics chose her fourth in the 2002 WNBA Draft. She didn't play much in two seasons. She was traded to Connecticut. At first the Sun didn't use her often either. Jones finally moved into the starting lineup in 2007. She became one of the team's most dependable scorers and was a two-time All-Star. Off the court, Jones launched a shoe brand for women with shoe sizes 10 to 15. It can be hard for women to find stylish footwear that large.

She gave the team a strong presence under the basket at both ends of the court. Connecticut swept Detroit in the first round. They defeated the Indiana Fever in the conference finals. Now they faced the Sacramento Monarchs in the WNBA Finals. Sacramento won the first game of the best-of-five series. The Sun won the next game in overtime. The Monarchs edged Connecticut in the next two games to become WNBA champions.

Connecticut won 26 games again in 2006. It was the league's best record. One reason was the improved play of forward Asjha Jones. She averaged 11 points a game. The Sun beat the Mystics in the first round. They faced Detroit in the conference finals. The teams split the first two games. It was all Shock in the third game. Detroit routed the Sun 79–55 to win the series.

TIME FOR A CHANGE

Connecticut couldn't repeat its regular season success in 2007. The team posted just a 5–10 mark by late June. They rallied to finish 18–16. They faced Indiana in the first round of the playoffs. Game 1 was the first triple-overtime game in league history. Connecticut held the Fever scoreless in the final minutes of the third overtime to win 93–88. Indiana easily won Game 2. The Sun built a 22-point lead in the deciding Game 3. They couldn't hold it. The game went to overtime again. The teams flipped their Game 1 scores. Indiana won 93–88. Douglas scored 27 points in her final game with the Sun.

The team traded Douglas before the 2008 season. They also played without Sales and Dydek. A losing record seemed likely. Yet Connecticut bolted to an 8–1 record to open the season. They finished 21–13. Thibault was named WNBA Coach of the Year again. The Sun faced the Liberty in the first round of the playoffs. New York won the first game. Connecticut won the second. The Liberty edged the Sun in the decisive Game 3, 66–62.

The Sun fell to 16–18 in 2009. They missed the playoffs for the first time since moving to Connecticut. A trade brought in guard Renee Montgomery before the 2010 season. She averaged more than 13 points a game. The Sun also had the first overall choice in the 2010 WNBA Draft. They took standout UConn center Tina Charles. Despite these additions, Connecticut finished 17–17. They missed the playoffs for the second year in a row. The Sun rebounded in 2011 to a 21–13 record. The Atlanta Dream swept them in the conference semifinals. The Sun held narrow leads going into the fourth quarter in both games but couldn't hang on.

Connecticut went 25–9 in 2012. Charles became the first Sun player to win the WNBA Most Valuable Player (MVP) award. The Sun swept the Liberty in the conference semifinals. They defeated Indiana in the first game of the conference finals. But the Fever edged them in Game 2, 78–76, on a jump shot with half a second remaining. Indiana cruised to an 87–71 series-clinching victory in Game 3.

Despite Thibault's excellent regular season record, he was fired. "Mike has had much success here in Connecticut over the past 10 seasons," said team official Chris Sienko. "However, we felt it was time for a new voice and new direction for our players and our fans as we continue to try to capture that first, elusive title."

Renee Montgomery

TINA CHARLES
CENTER
HEIGHT: 6-FOOT-4
SUN SEASONS: 2010–13

TINA'S BIG NIGHT

In the second half of UConn's game against Notre Dame on March 1, 2010, Tina Charles scored her 13th point. That made her the school's all-time leading scorer. She surpassed Nykesha Sales. Her fifth rebound in the same game gave her the school's career rebound record as well. "That's just a weird coincidence, it really is," said coach Geno Auriemma. Charles is the only player in school history to hold both records at the same time. Not surprisingly, the Sun made Charles the top overall draft choice shortly afterward. She justified the team's confidence. She was WNBA Rookie of the Year in 2010, All-WNBA First Team in 2011 and 2012, and the Sun's first WNBA MVP in 2012.

BE CAREFUL WHAT YOU WISH FOR

That "new voice" belonged to veteran coach Anne Donovan. She had led Seattle to the WNBA title in 2004. She also coached the 2008 U.S. Olympic gold medal-winning team. But the "new direction" that management hoped for was downward rather than up. In 2013, Donovan's first season, she had to deal with a series of injuries to important players. There was another problem. Some players had a hard time dealing with Donovan's new system. The team lost seven of their first eight games. Things never really got better. The Sun finished 10–24. It is the worst record in team history.

The Sun improved to 13–19 in 2014. Douglas returned for her final WNBA season. Two rookies did especially well. Forward/center Chiney Ogwumike was the first overall draft choice. She averaged more than 15 points and 8 rebounds a game. Forward Alyssa Thomas averaged 10 points and 5 rebounds a game. Both were named to the WNBA All-Rookie First Team.

Unfortunately, Ogwumike missed all of the 2015 season due to injury. Other players missed parts of the season with injuries. The Sun finished 15–19, even though they started with a 7–1 record. One bright spot was center Kelsey Bone's 31-point outing in the season's final game. "I think it is important for our fans, a reminder for who we have been and who we will be moving forward," Donovan said. She wouldn't be a part of the "moving forward," though. She resigned soon after the season ended.

Donovan's replacement, Curt Miller, couldn't reverse the team's slide in 2016. Connecticut finished just 14–20. Things improved in 2017 even though the team lost their first four games. They battled back to finish 21–13. That record earned them a first-round bye in the playoffs. They faced the Phoenix Mercury in the one-game second round. The score was tied at the end of the third quarter. The Mercury outscored the Sun 20–15 in the final quarter. Despite that setback, Miller was named WNBA Coach of the Year.

The situation was virtually identical in 2018. The Sun won 9 of their final 10 games. They finished 21–13 again. They had a first-round bye. They met Phoenix in the second round. Phoenix won, 96–86.

THE SUN RISING IN THE EAST

The Sun's 23–11 record in 2019 earned them byes in the first two rounds of the playoffs. They faced the Los Angeles Sparks in the best-of-five semifinal round. Connecticut notched their first playoff victory in seven years with an 84–73 win in Game 1. They crushed the Sparks 94–68 in Game 2 and 78–56 in Game 3.

That put the Sun in the WNBA Finals for the first time in 14 years. They faced the top-seeded Mystics. Washington's coach was . . . Mike Thibault. The teams traded victories in the first four games of the best-of-five series. Connecticut had a two-point lead after the third quarter in Game 5. Washington outscored them 27-14 in the fourth quarter. The Mystics won 89–78.

Alyssa Thomas

A WOMAN OF FIRSTS

Chiney Ogwumike graduated from Stanford University as the Pac-12's career scoring leader between both sexes. The Sun made her the first overall choice of the 2014 WNBA Draft. She averaged more than 15 points and 7 rebounds per game. She was named WNBA Rookie of the Year. Ogwumike and her sister Nneka (who plays for Los Angeles) became the first pair of sisters named to the All-Star Game. She missed all of 2015 due to a knee injury. After returning in 2016, she missed 2017 due to another injury. She had another All-Star season in 2018. Then she was traded to the Sparks. In 2020, she became the first Black woman to host a national radio show for ESPN.

CHINEY OGWUMIKE
FORWARD/CENTER
HEIGHT: 6-FOOT-3
SUN SEASONS: 2014–18

CONNECTICUT SUN

Because of the COVID-19 pandemic, the 2020 season was shortened to 22 games. All the games were played in Bradenton, Florida. There were no spectators. The Sun finished 10–12. They still qualified for the playoffs. They pulled away to beat the Chicago Sky 94–81 in the first round. The Sun outscored Los Angeles 22–8 in the first quarter in the second round. They cruised to a 73–59 victory. Now they faced the Las Vegas Aces in the best-of-five semifinals. The teams split the first four games. Las Vegas eked out a 66–63 win in Game 5.

The WNBA returned to a normal schedule in 2021. Connecticut finished the season with a 14-game winning streak. That gave them a league-best 26 victories. It matched the team's best-ever win total. Miller received his second WNBA Coach of the Year award. The Sun had byes in the first two rounds. They faced the 16–16 Chicago Sky in the semifinals. Connecticut was heavily favored. But Chicago won Game 1 in double overtime, 101–95. Connecticut rebounded to win Game 2. Chicago won Game 3, as the Sun missed two potential game-tying shots in the final moments. The Sky closed out the series with a 79–69 win in Game 4. It is one of the biggest upsets in WNBA history.

The Sun also made a bit of dubious history. It was the first time that the No. 1 overall seed hadn't reached the WNBA Finals since the league changed its playoff format in 2016. "It's certainly a sad and disappointed locker room," Miller said. "It's just a disappointing eight-day stretch where we just were out-coached, we were out-played. It just felt like we were always on our heels this series."

JONQUEL JONES
FORWARD
HEIGHT: 6-FOOT-6
SUN SEASONS: 2016-22

FAST BLOOMER

The Los Angeles Sparks chose Jonquel Jones as the No. 6 overall pick in the 2016 WNBA Draft. They traded her to Connecticut. She had a slow start, averaging fewer than seven points per game as a rookie. She quickly improved. Jones doubled her scoring average per game in the following season. She also pulled down nearly 12 rebounds per game. "She is one of the most versatile and talented players in the world," coach Curt Miller said. Jones was named the league's MVP in 2021. She averaged more than 11 rebounds per game to lead the league. Her average of 19.4 points per game ranked fourth.

CONNECTICUT SUN

Courtney Williams

There was another disappointment. In 2021, the WNBA had begun a mini-tournament called the Commissioners Cup. The first home and first away games against the other five teams in the conference counted in the standings. The Sun's 9–1 record led the Eastern Conference standings. But they lost to the Western Conference-leading Storm, 79–57.

The Sun spent the 2022 season near the top of the standings. They finished 25–11. After missing nearly all of the previous season, Alyssa Thomas was named to the All-Star team for the third time. She was also named to the All-WNBA and All-Defensive Teams. Connecticut won the best-of-three first round series over the Dallas Wings, 2 games to 1. They split the first four games with Chicago in the best-of-five semifinals. Trailing by 10 points in the fourth quarter in the decisive Game 5, the Sun scored the final 18 points to emerge with a 72–63 win. It is the longest run to close out a playoff game in league history.

The Sun faced Las Vegas in the WNBA Finals. A potential game-tying three-point shot fell short as Las Vegas held on for a 67–64 victory in Game 1. The Aces won Game 2 as well. The Sun routed the Aces in Game 3, 105–76. Game 4 was tied at 67 with three minutes left. But Las Vegas pulled away for a 78–71 victory. Once again, the Sun fell short of the title.

The Connecticut Sun has been one of the WNBA's most successful franchises. After a four-season string in the mid-2010s where they missed the playoffs, they have been a fixture in the postseason since then. Fans hope that the team will finally capture the elusive championship.

Natisha Hiedeman

INDEX